GW01091518

"To trust the spirit of our loving God deep within is a lifelong ¡
Dear Child is a wonderful guide that helps children grow in this process. Deborah Roslak and Linda Orber have provided an appealing guide by which children are led to prayer; they are encouraged to listen and speak honestly not only in letter form, but in quiet meditations where they are 'in touch' with their friend Jesus. I recommend this book not only as a fine resource for parents and teachers, but as background for homilists addressing children."

Bernice Stadler
Co-author, *Celebrations of the Word for Children*

"Having worked in preschool and kindergarten religious education, I know the importance of early religious attitudinal development. We must help children touch Jesus at an early age, and this book provides an excellent tool for praying with young elementary school children. *Dear Jesus, Dear Child* takes their own experiences and helps them find Jesus present there and within themselves.

"Adults using this book with their students will be touched with the Spirit of Jesus too. To become 'as children' and to relate to Jesus in the childlike manner set forth in this book will serve to begin or deepen the adult's relationship with Jesus. As always, when 'teaching' children, one learns much more than one imparts!

"I look forward to using this resource in our parish's elementary religious education program."

Karen Leslie
DRE and author, *Faith and Little Children: A Guide for Parents and Teachers*

"What a creative and charming way to make children aware of God's loving presence! As they hear their real concerns voiced in letters to Jesus and listen to his response, they receive insight into their problems. More important, through these letters and the guided meditations that follow, children will come to know Jesus as friend and helper. They will be more likely to turn to him spontaneously for the rest of their lives.

"This book helps us foster in children a strong relationship with God built on trust and love—the greatest gift we can give them."

Sr. M. Kathleen Glavich, S.N.D.
Catechist, author
General editor of the *Christ Our Life* Series

DEAR JESUS DEAR CHILD

Guided Meditations for Young Children

Deborah Roslak and Linda Joy Orber

TWENTY-THIRD PUBLICATIONS

Mystic, Connecticut 06355

Illustrations by William Baker

Twenty-Third Publications
P.O. Box 180
185 Willow Street
Mystic, CT 06355
(203) 536-2611
800-321-0411

ISBN: 0-89622-508-9
Library of Congress Catalog Card No. 91-67713

PREFACE

Dear Jesus, Dear Child: Guided Meditations for Young Children was created to help parents, catechists, and teachers help their children to learn and experience the love and security deep inside them. Children have many fears, many questions, and many concerns. This book was designed as a way for the caring adults in their lives to help children acknowledge their concerns and feelings and answer them with love.

We present Jesus in a very gentle, tender, and loving way since that is our own continuing experience of him. We believe that children can grow up with that experience, too.

The first letter in each section of this book is written by an imaginary child and addressed to Jesus. We believe each letter acknowledges how children really think and feel inside, but may not be able to express it. So the children writing the letters speak for them. Their fears are the fears of all of us. The responses from "Jesus" incorporate not only some practical advice, but teach children that there is another way to look at things, and that they have a wonderful friend whose love is always there to help them.

The guided prayer meditations offer children an opportunity to experience love, peace, and caring directly, since they are written in a very gentle, loving way. We hope that the adults who lead the meditations will read them slowly and very lovingly. We also hope parents, catechists, and teachers will feel free to ad lib where they feel they need to, and eventually begin to create their own meditations.

The illustrated pages—meant for coloring—help children imagine themselves in gentle and safe places where they can feel close to Jesus. There is also space on each of these pages for them to create their own prayer to Jesus. Through this process they learn that they can feel free to speak to Jesus in their own words and in their own way. This kind of personal prayer helps children deepen their experience of Jesus' love and care.

Our goal is to help children discover for themselves that there is a very real place inside of them where they can go to find the help they need. We want them to know that there is always someone with them who loves them very much. These are experiences that can be strengthened as the child develops and grows.

We hope each child can learn to depend on the love inside them, and learn to listen to a voice that speaks with gentleness and peace.

DEDICATION

With much love we dedicate this book to our children

Eddie and Elizabeth Roslak
Alissa and Jordan Orber

who truly sparked our quest to find a gentle, loving way in which to teach them of the love that lives and grows within them.

We would also like to acknowledge Linda Nilsen, principal of Trinity Lutheran School, and Virginia Savarese, principal of St. Mary's School, both of Staten Island, New York, whose need to reach out in love inspired the ideas in this book. Their care and concern for the healthy spiritual growth of their students allowed the children in their schools to touch the tremendous power of guidance and love that lives within us all.

It is to the needs of these children and all children that the Voice of Love so gently speaks.

CONTENTS

DEAR JESUS DEAR CHILD

1. DOES GOD ANSWER MY PRAYER?

Dear Jesus,

Today was my birthday, but I'm not very happy. For the past month I prayed real hard every night for a bicycle. I promised to be good forever. I promised not to fight with my brothers and sisters. I promised to clean my room if only I could have this one thing.

When I finished opening up all my presents there was no bicycle. So, I figure either one of two things—either God is mad at me for something, or God never heard my prayers at all.

Do you think that you can ask God about this? Because I don't think my prayers are being heard.

Thank you.

Love,

Jimmy

Dear Jimmy,

I can see how badly you wanted that bicycle. I'm
sorry you're sad. It's just that your parents don't have
the money for a bike just now. God is not angry at
you, and neither am I. You haven't done anything wrong,
and we love you very much. So do your parents.

You have to understand, Jimmy, that I came to bring
something special into the world, and that something
is peace.

I know a bicycle would make you happy for a little
while. But then you would want something else to make
you happy. You would never learn that real happiness
comes from inside of you. That is the place I came to
remind everyone of.

Also, since your mom and dad can't get you that bike
right now, maybe you can think of ways to try and get
it yourself. Maybe you can do some work to earn the
money for the bike. We can talk about it together,
and I can help you with some ideas. It's okay to try and
help yourself.

Remember that if you don't get what you ask for, it's
never because God is angry with you. Sometimes it
just works out that way. But I'll always be with you to
help you to learn that happiness is inside of you,
because love is inside of you. I'll always be with you.

Love,
Jesus

Guided Meditation

It is a quiet and gentle place. Goodness lives there. No anger, no sadness, or worry could ever frighten away the goodness in this place. *Pause.*

Love lives there. There we can live and grow and know that we are always safe. *Pause.*

This is the place where Jesus lives. It is inside each and every one of you. No matter who you are, what you look like, or what you have or don't have, this place is in you. *Pause .*

Find that wonderful place within you now. Imagine that you see Jesus there. *Pause.*

See Jesus coming to meet you? Look how happy he is to see you! *Pause.*

He's standing with you now. His eyes are gentle and kind. You can see that he loves you. He is smiling at you now. His smile makes you feel safe. *Pause.*

Listen to what Jesus is saying to you now. What is he telling you? *Pause.*

Perhaps Jesus is saying something like this to you:

Dearest child,
I am so very happy that you are here with me now. I want you to know that whenever you need me, and need to feel my love, all you need do is come here to this special place inside of you. I will always be here with you. I will never leave you. I will always love you, for all of your life. *Longer pause.*

What would you like to say to Jesus? *Longer pause.*

Now, in a moment, you're going to open your eyes. But when you do, you're going to remember the wonderful way you felt knowing that Jesus is always with you, and that he loves you.

You're also going to remember that you are never alone. Jesus is always with you, loving you, no matter what.

Now slowly begin to open your eyes.

Let us pray...

Jesus, we know we are never alone. You live within each of us, smiling within us, loving us. Thank you, Jesus, for always being with us, and thank you for loving each one of us so much. Amen.

My prayer to Jesus

2. I WANT MY ALLOWANCE!

Dear Jesus,

A few months ago my mother made a list of all the chores that I would be responsible for around the house. She said if I did all my jobs, on Thursdays I would get an allowance.

Well, this was okay by me, because I like getting an allowance. But my mom just told me this morning that she won't be able to pay me my allowance for a while. She says she just doesn't have enough money.

Jesus, do I still have to do my jobs, even for no allowance? I told my mom that I didn't want to work for nothing, and I'm kind of angry that she isn't going to pay me. But there's another part of me that sort of feels guilty for feeling this way.

Please help me figure this out, Jesus.

Love,

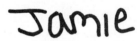

Dear Jamie,

There are many ways that people get "paid" for the work they do. Students get good grades on their report card for their hard work in school. People who volunteer in hospitals or libraries get paid by the good feelings they have when they help others who need them.

My best "pay" was knowing that I was helping others to remember that they were loved, no matter who they were or what their behavior had been. This for me, was the best "pay" of all.

If you do all the chores your mom asks you to do, Jamie, you will indeed get "paid" for them, though maybe not with money. First of all, your mom will be grateful for the help that you give, and that will make her happy.

Maybe she will have extra time then to spend talking with you or helping you in some way. Perhaps she will have extra time to bake or cook something special that you and your family enjoy.

Everybody wins when they work together, Jamie. Then all the love inside of them is given a chance to grow and shine. We all get "paid" when we share our love with others.

Love,
Jesus

Guided Meditation

Let's close our eyes and take a deep breath. Breathe in deeply and exhale slowly.

Now take another deep breath, really deep this time, and then let out all the air. *Pause.*

In a few moments, we're going to visit that special place inside us that God created. It's a place full of love and joy. *Pause*

With your eyes closed, imagine you're in a beautiful place that makes you feel happy and safe. It doesn't matter where. It can be some place you've been to or some place you can make up, like a quiet spot in a garden, under a big tree in a grassy meadow, or in an apple orchard. It can be any place you would like. *Long pause.*

Now with your eyes closed, imagine how your special place looks, and how safe and happy it makes you feel. *Long pause.*

Imagine now in your favorite lovely spot that Jesus is coming toward you. *Pause.*

Just call him quietly in your mind. He wants you to call him because he loves you and wants to spend time with you. *Pause.*

If you like, imagine that Jesus is hugging you or holding you. Imagine whatever feels comfortable. *Long pause.*

Now that Jesus is with you, it's all right to share with him how you feel when you're with him. If you like, you can tell him how much you love him and how it feels to be with him. *Pause.*

Jesus loves you and wants you to tell him about all your feelings, the unhappy ones and the happy ones, too. He wants to hear all about your love for him. *Pause.*

Jesus rejoices each time you open your heart. The more you open your heart to his love, the more he can fill it. *Pause.*

Quietly, in your mind, tell Jesus about the loving feelings you have for him. He loves you and wants to hear all about them. *Long pause.*

Now that you've shared with Jesus all about your love, he wants to share his love with you. *Pause.*

If you want to, you can let Jesus hold you while he's telling you all about his love. *Pause.*

Quietly, in your mind listen to what Jesus has to say to you, perhaps something like this:

My little child,
I love you so very much. I will always be with you in this place of love within your heart. Whenever you need to, you can come to this quiet place and let me tell you how much you mean to me. You are my little child and I will always be with you. *Long pause.*

It's all right to be with Jesus for a few more moments. It feels so good to be with him. *Pause.*

You're going to open your eyes in a moment. But when you do, remember how much Jesus loves you, and that he'll always be with you to help you, to talk to or to just give you a hug. *Pause.*

Quietly, now open your eyes.

Let us pray...

Jesus, thank you for all the love you share with us, and for helping us to open our hearts and share our love with you and others. Amen.

My prayer to Jesus

_____

_____

_____

_____

_____

3. MY PARENTS DON'T LOVE ME!

Dear Jesus,

Today I feel so terrible. Jennifer's parents bought
her a new dress and new shoes and a new headband. It
wasn't like it was her birthday or anything. It was
for no reason at all. I was jealous and felt bad,
because she's always getting new things. It seems
like all she has to do is ask for something, and poof,
she has it.

Jesus, I don't want to feel jealous, because it
doesn't feel good, but I never get new things "for
no reason at all."

Sometimes I think that maybe Jennifer's parents
love her more than mine love me, although my mom and
dad are really nice. I love them a whole lot
(except when they yell at me!). Could it really be
true that her parents love her more than mine love
me?

Could it be true that you love her more, too? I
really don't understand this. Can you help me?

Love,

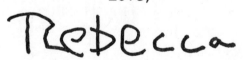

Rebecca

Dear Rebecca,

I can understand that it seems like someone else (or everyone else) has things that are much better or more important than you.

This is difficult to understand, Rebecca, even for grown-ups, so listen carefully, and listen with your heart. Comparing yourself to others is a waste of time! You will always feel either that they are better than you, or that you are better than them. Neither of these feelings will make you truly happy. One feeling leads you to believe that you are missing something inside of yourself, and the other leads you to believe that someone else is missing something.

Rebecca, as you look around you will notice that different people all have more or less of this thing or that. That's just how it is. I want you to always remember this though: You and everyone in the world have all of my love and the love of God. The more you share this love the bigger it grows. It is the only thing you can keep giving away and still not have less of it.

Don't judge your parents, my dear, by how many things they are able to give you. Just concentrate on sharing all the love in your heart. And that, you will learn, is what really matters.

Love,
Jesus

Guided Meditation

Close your eyes and take a very deep breath. Exhale slowly. *Pause.*

Let's take another deep breath and exhale. *Pause.*

Now find the special place inside you where love is. Feel how wonderful God's love is. Feel how peaceful it is just to rest in this love. *Pause.*

Imagine yourself with Jesus in your quiet loving place. Imagine being with him in whatever way makes you feel happy. *Long pause.*

As you sit safely with Jesus, feeling all of his love, you can begin to think about something you need or want. Perhaps it's something you can't have right away. Perhaps it upsets you that you can't have it right now. *Pause.*

Tell Jesus about it and how it makes you feel. He would like to help you feel better. *Longer Pause.*

Jesus loves you and wants you to feel peaceful inside. Now that you have told him how you feel, you can begin to let him help you. *Pause.*

Jesus understands that sometimes having things is important to you. But he also knows that even if you can't have it right now, you do have something much more important. You have all of his love. Jesus knows that love is really what makes people feel happy and joyful, because love is forever. *Pause.*

With your eyes closed, listen quietly to what Jesus has to say to you. He loves you and wants you to remember that you have all of his love and that's really what's important. *Pause.*

Perhaps you will hear Jesus say something like this to you:

Dearest child,
I love you so very much. Even though there are many things in the world you think you want or need, try to remember that God gives you the most important gift of all. You have all of God's love and all of mine. Whenever you feel bad, you can let yourself feel this love and know that God is with you, loving you so very much. *Longer pause.*

It's okay now to be with Jesus and feel how much he loves you and how much he cares for you. *Longer pause.*

In a few moments it will be time to open our eyes and return to this place. But you can take Jesus' love with you. *Pause.*

You can remember too, that you have what's really important, and that God's love is always with you. Jesus is always here to help you to remember how very much you are loved. *Pause.*

Quietly, now open your eyes.

||||||||||||||||||||||||||||||||||||||||||||||||||||||||||||||||||||||||||||||||||||||||||||||||||||||||||||||||||||||||||||||

Let us pray...

Jesus, thank you for reminding us that we already have what is truly important, that your love and God's love is ours, always and forever. Amen.

My prayer to Jesus

_____

_____

_____

_____

_____

Dear Jesus,

I've had this problem for a few weeks now. I've tried to solve it myself, but it's just getting worse.

There's another girl in my class who picks on me. She waits for me to get on the school bus, and then she starts to call me names. She makes fun of anything I wear or say.

The only time she'll stop is when I give her half my lunch. Then when it's lunchtime, I'm really hungry because there's not much left to eat.

She has even shoved me around a few times. I want to be grown-up about this, Jesus, but I need all the help you can give me.

Thank you.

Love,

Patricia

Dear Patricia,

Some people (even grown-ups) find all different kinds
of ways to bully other people. Do you know why they act
this way?

They do it because they are afraid themselves! They're
afraid that there is something that they are missing
inside of themselves, and that they must get that
something by taking it away from someone else.

The first thing to remember, Patricia, is that no one
in the whole world is really missing anything inside
of them. That would mean that God created love for some
people and not for others! God created the same love
inside of every one of us. But some of God's children
have forgotten that it is there.

The best way to stop the bully in your class is to help
her stop her teasing. Don't be afraid to tell your
parents, your teacher, and if you have to, the
principal of your school. This will be the most
loving act that you can do to help her.

Remember, too, Patricia, that I am always with you,
and my love is inside of you and everyone around you.
No one can ever steal that love away. I'll do my best
to help you remember this love within you. All that you
need to do is be willing to let me.

Love,

Jesus

Guided Meditation

Close your eyes, and then take a deep breath in and slowly exhale. Take another deep breath in, and as you let it go, feel your shoulders, your neck, your legs and feet completely relax. *Pause.*

Many times you have visited a special place of love inside yourself. It is a place of quiet and of happiness. Now in your mind, find the special place of love that you have visited before. This is the place of God's love, and the place where Jesus is always with you, to talk with you and listen to whatever you want to say to him. *Pause.*

Now, in your mind imagine that you see a beautiful blue light. *Pause.*

As you watch this beautiful, blue light, it becomes brighter and bigger. Soon the light is so wide and tall that it surrounds every corner of your mind. *Pause.*

Imagine now that you are standing in the center of this light, and that one by one everyone you have ever met and anyone you have ever known is stepping into it. *Pause.*

As more people step into this wonderful place, it becomes lighter and lighter until it sparkles and turns as white as white can be. *Pause.*

Everyone standing there has this wonderful white sparkling light all around them. This is the light of love, and the light of God, who knows only love. Everyone, all over the world, has all of God's love. No one is ever left out of that wonderful light. No one has more love than someone else. *Longer pause.*

Quietly, in your mind, tell Jesus how you feel standing in God's light with everyone. *Pause.*

Now listen to what Jesus answers you. *Longer pause.*

Perhaps Jesus is saying something like this to you:

Beloved child,
The light of love that you see in your mind is the light of God that you carry within your heart always. It is the light of love that God has for all of us. Whenever something confuses you or upsets you, try to remember that in your heart and in your mind is the light of God's love. Then ask God to help you to understand what confuses or upsets you. God's light will never leave you, and God's love will always be with you. *Longer pause.*

Take a deep breath in, and slowly exhale. In a moment you will open your eyes. But you will remember that you will always have the light of God's love in your heart. *Pause.*

Take another deep breath in, then slowly let it go. Now open your eyes.

Let us pray...

Jesus, thank you for helping us to see the light of love that shines in each of us. Help us to remember that everyone has this love in their hearts, and help us to appreciate that light in ourselves and each other. Amen.

My prayer to Jesus

5. I'M WORRIED ABOUT MY GRANDMA

Dear Jesus,

I'm very sad right now because my grandmother is very sick. My mother told me they have to take her to the hospital. Mom said that's the best place for my grandma, because they'll take good care of her there.

I'm very worried about her, Jesus. Grandma is getting kind of old. I'm real scared she won't get well.

I love her very much, Jesus; she's very special to me, and I know how much she loves me, too. Every Christmas she makes butter cookies just for me. She even gave me the locket she wore around her neck, one she has had since she was a little girl. She waited to give it to me because she wanted me to be able to take good care of it.

Jesus, please help my grandma. Could you help me, too?

Love,

Megan

Dear Megan,

I know how worried you are about your grandma, and
how much you want her to get well. I also know how
much you love her, and how much she loves you.

The best way I can help you, Megan, is to remind you
that even when things seem difficult, you have
inside of you all the love and safety God created.
That love and safety is always there, waiting to
be remembered and shared.

You can help yourself and your grandma by letting
me help you remember that love, and sharing it with
her.

When just one person remembers the light of love
inside him or her, that light grows and grows.
Even though people might not show it, somewhere
inside their hearts they remember, too.

Megan, I'm always here with you, and with your
grandma. Let me help you to remember the love we
share, and that love will help her too.

Love,

Jesus

Guided Meditation

Close your eyes and take a deep breath in and then exhale slowly. Take another deep breath and exhale. *Pause.*

Deep inside of us is the gentle light of love that God created. Today we are going to remember that love and share it and watch it grow. *Pause.*

With your eyes closed, imagine yourself surrounded by a beautiful, glowing white light. Perhaps at first, it doesn't seem very bright to you. But imagine it grows brighter and more beautiful as you feel more and more loving. *Longer pause.*

Imagine now that as you are surrounded by that beautiful light, you see Jesus. He is surrounded by a wonderful glorious light, too. *Longer pause.*

Imagine now that Jesus is waiting for you to come into his light. You can imagine that he's waiting for you. He's holding his arms out to you and is looking at you with all the love in his heart. *Longer pause.*

If you like, imagine yourself walking into his loving, gentle light. Notice how much bigger and more beautiful the light is when you both share it. Imagine that loving light is so wonderful, and makes you feel so happy and safe, that you can't help but want to share it. *Pause.*

Think now of someone you want to invite in to share the light of love that you and Jesus now share together. *Longer pause.*

You can invite someone who hasn't been feeling well, or someone who seems unhappy. Or just someone you think needs some special love. *Longer pause.*

Imagine, too, that the glowing light is helping that person to feel safe and loved, and so much better inside. *Longer pause.*

With your eyes closed, imagine Jesus telling you how happy he is that you're willing to share your loving light with someone else. He is also happy that you are letting him share his light with you. *Pause.*

Perhaps you hear Jesus say something like this:

My little child,
Thank you so very much for letting me share my light and love with you. Thank you so much for sharing yours. God created that love to be shared. Every time you share it, you help others to remember all the wonderful love that is inside them. I love you very much, and I'm so grateful for all the love you willingly share. I'm always here to share all of my love with you. *Longer pause.*

In a moment we're going to open our eyes. When we do, we can remember all the love inside of us that Jesus wants us to share. We can also remember he is always with us to help us. *Pause.*

Now let's quietly open our eyes.

Let us pray...

Thank you, Jesus, for helping us to remember the gentle light of love that surrounds us, and lives in our hearts. Help us to share that beautiful light with everyone around us as they try to remember all the love within them, too. Amen.

My prayer to Jesus

6. I'M TIRED OF FIGHTING!

Dear Jesus,

My big sister is always pushing me around. It sure makes me mad. Did you make her the boss or something?

My little brother is just as much trouble. He gets into my room and messes up all my stuff. When I yell at him I get into trouble.

Sometimes I wish they would just disappear, so I wouldn't have to share my things. I wouldn't have to listen to my big sister, and I wouldn't have to fight and argue with my brother.

My mom and dad always seem to be on their side. They say that we should love one another because we're brothers and sisters. I don't think they understand how hard that is to do.

I sure would appreciate your help.

Love,

Katherine

Dear Katherine,

I understand how angry you feel when your big
sister bosses you around, and when your little
brother comes in and messes up your room. It
certainly seems unfair.

You're angry, too, that you're not getting more
attention from your mom and dad. The others seem to
be taking time away from you.

But you know what, Katherine? You forgot that I'm
always here with you. When you're jealous of your
sister and brother you can remember that you're not
alone. Maybe your parents don't have time, all the
time, for you, but I always do. You can talk to me
anytime. I'm always here to listen.

Sometimes brothers and sisters act in ways we don't
like, and it makes us angry. It's okay to tell
your sister not to be bossy with you, or to tell your
brother not to mess up your things. But try to say
it with love.

I had to tell people not to do things that were
destructive and hurtful, but I always tried to do it
with love and compassion. Every time you act with
love, Katherine, it helps you to remember about all
the love inside of you, and it will make you
happy.

Love,
Jesus

Guided Meditation

Close your eyes and be very still. *Pause.*

Take a deep breath in and then exhale slowly. *Pause.*

Now take another deep breath and exhale. *Pause.*

Now you are going to remember that deep inside you is a very peaceful and lovely place. It's the place where Jesus lives. Today we're going to visit that special place again. *Pause.*

Feel how quiet and still everything is, and how peaceful. *Pause.*

In this quiet place deep inside of you, Jesus waits for you to hear him calling you. Can you hear him calling your name? *Pause.*

He's putting his arms around you, and you feel very safe now. You're not afraid of anything because you're with Jesus, and he loves you so very much. *Pause.*

Just feel how wonderful and safe it is to be with him in his arms. *Pause.*

Tell him now about anything that is bothering you. Tell him about your sisters and brothers and how you feel about them. You can be honest with Jesus because he loves and understands how you feel. *Longer pause.*

Listen quietly to what you can hear Jesus saying to you. *Pause.*

Perhaps you heard Jesus say something like this to you:

My little child,
I love you. I am always with you. Whenever you're upset or afraid, you can come to this quiet place and let me hold you until you feel safe again. I'm always here waiting for you. I love you. I'll be with you forever. *Longer pause.*

Now quietly in your mind tell Jesus how you feel. Maybe you can feel him hug you and hear him tell you how much he loves you. *Pause.*

You're going to open your eyes now in a minute. And you're going to remember that Jesus is with you and you can let him hold you whenever you need to. And you'll always know that you're never alone.

Now slowly begin to open your eyes.

||||||||||||||||||||||||||||||||||||||||||||||||||||||||||||||||||||||||||||||||||||||||||||||||||||||||||

Let us pray...

Jesus, we know that you are with us now, and that you love us. Help us to remember that we can come to you whenever we need to. Help us to remember that we're never alone, and that you are always with us. Amen.

My prayer to Jesus

_____

_____

_____

_____

_____

Dear Jesus,

Today I'm not allowed to go out and play. I'm being punished. I know my dad told me not to go off the block without telling him. But I was in a hurry, and I just ran around the corner with Matt. Boy, was dad mad when he couldn't find me! Now I'm stuck in the house after school for two days.

Jesus, does God punish people, too? Sometimes I think if something bad happens, maybe it's because God is punishing me for something I did or something I forgot about. After all, God is a father, too. If God is like my dad, I'm in big trouble.

Love,

Mike

Dear Mike,

I know you're upset about being punished, and I know that you're worried about whether God will punish you.

First of all, Mike, let me tell you what God is like. God is always loving. That's because God is love. We were created to be loving and happy with God forever.

God doesn't punish people. That's what I came to teach. God is always forgiving, even when it's hard for us to forgive ourselves, or others. We can try and remember that God has already forgiven us.

Sometimes bad things do happen, but this is not because God is angry at anyone. It's just the way life is sometimes. But God is always there, like I am, to help you to feel better and remember how much you are loved and treasured, even when things around you seem upsetting.

I'm sorry you were punished for not listening to your dad, Mike. But try and remember that your dad was worried when he couldn't find you. He loves you and wants to keep you safe. I will help you to forgive your dad, just as God has forgiven you.

Love,

Jesus

Guided Meditation

In a few moments we're going to visit that special place of love inside of us that God created. *Pause.*

Take a deep breath in, and then exhale slowly. Now take another breath, very deep this time and exhale. *Pause.*

With your eyes closed, imagine for a moment a place filled with beautiful golden light. *Pause.*

Jesus is standing in the center of this light. He's standing with his arms open wide and with a loving smile. He loves you, and wants you to come to him. *Pause.*

If you want to, you can run into his arms, or just hold his hand. Imagine whatever feels comfortable and makes you happy. *Pause.*

You can just quietly sit for a moment and be with Jesus in all the beautiful golden light. *Pause.*

Quietly now in your mind, tell Jesus anything you feel bad about. It could be something you said or did, or a thought you had that made you feel bad. Jesus loves you and wants to help you feel better and to know that you're forgiven. *Long pause.*

Now that you have told Jesus what is bothering you, you can let him help you to feel better and know how much he loves you. *Pause.*

In your mind, listen quietly and imagine what Jesus would say to you that would help you know how much he loves you, and how much you are forgiven. *Pause.*

Perhaps Jesus wants to say something like this to you:

My little child,
I love you so very much. I know that sometimes you think or say or do something you feel bad about. But I want you to know that God loves you and forgives you. God wants you to forgive yourself. I want you to feel better and to know that I am always with you, loving you. God is love, and love always forgives. Love is always gentle, and kind. Our love is always with you. *Long pause.*

Now that you've listened to Jesus, perhaps you can just rest a moment and feel how very much he cares for you. *Long pause.*

We're going to open our eyes in a few moments. Let's remember when we do how much Jesus loves us. We can also remember that whenever we feel bad, we can come to Jesus and talk about it. We can let him help us to feel better and know that we're loved and forgiven. *Pause.*

When we're ready, let's open our eyes.

Let us pray...

Jesus, help us to remember that God's forgiveness is always with us. Help us to remember that we can forgive others as well, since love is gentle and always forgiving.

Amen.

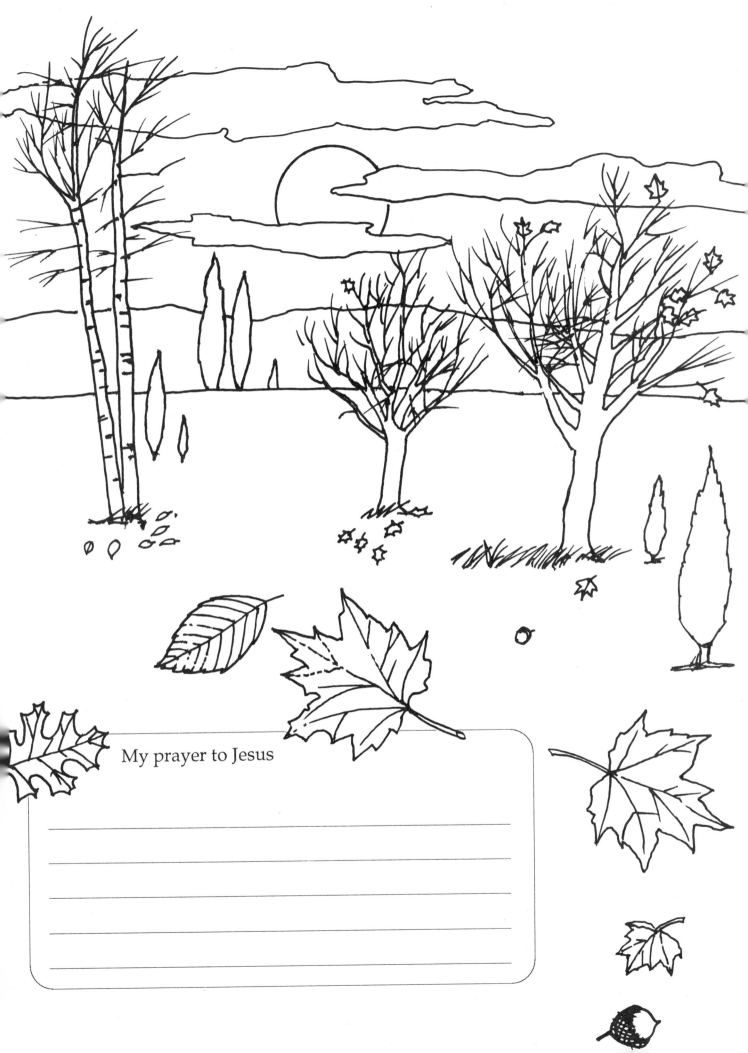

My prayer to Jesus

_____

_____

_____

_____

_____

8. I'M WORRIED ABOUT EARTH

Dear Jesus,

In school we are learning and talking about Earth
and how dirty the environment is getting. My teacher
told us that if people aren't careful, many plants
and animals could become extinct.

I feel very bad about this. I feel bad, too, when
I see people not seeming to care about this problem.
The oceans are getting polluted with oil spills
and garbage, and it's getting harder and harder for
plants and animals to live.

Sometimes I think maybe God is angry that we messed
everything up. If God is angry, Jesus, could you
say we're sorry?

Love,

Dear Peter,

I know how badly you feel about the way Earth is being treated. I also understand that you're worried that God is angry.

I want very much to help you with this. First of all, Peter, God isn't angry about it. But God does want all of us to live in a world where we feel safe and happy. This helps us to remember that God's love is always there, being reflected in the world around us.

God is a perfect loving Father and cares very much about us. When we love and care for another, whether it's a plant, an animal, or a person, we are teaching ourselves how much God loves us. You see, Peter, God created all the love inside you. Sharing that love is a way to learn that God is always sharing love with you. By the way, Peter, the best way to teach other people about caring is by demonstrating how loving and caring you can be.

That's what I came to teach, and you can teach it, too.

Love,

Jesus

Guided Meditation

Close your eyes and take a deep breath. Now take another deep breath and exhale slowly. *Pause.*

Quietly with our eyes closed, we're going to remember all the gentle love inside of us, and share that love and gentle caring with the life around us. *Pause.*

With your eyes closed, imagine yourself in a beautiful garden. Look around you at all the beautiful plants, flowers, bushes, and trees. *Pause.*

You can have a garden that's filled, not only with plants and flowers, but perhaps with birds and animals, too. *Pause.*

Imagine whatever makes you happy and gives you a sense of deep peace. *Pause.*

Now quietly in your mind, invite Jesus into your beautiful garden. *Pause.*

You can show him all of the plants and flowers that you have, and share with him your joy and your love. *Longer pause.*

Jesus is glad that you invited him into your garden, and he smiles in joy at all the love you have to share. *Pause.*

Now with your eyes still closed, look carefully around your garden, and choose one flower that you think needs special care. *Longer pause.*

Bring that flower to Jesus. He will help you to give it love. *Pause.*

Jesus wants to show you how important it is to share your love. *Pause.*

Together with Jesus give your flower as much love as you can. Feel yourself sending out your love to your flower. *Pause.*

Now imagine that as you give all your love to your flower that it begins to respond to your love and to grow and bloom more beautifully than ever. *Pause.*

Imagine too, that Jesus is gently helping you as he shares his love with you and everything around him. *Pause.*

Imagine now that Jesus wants to speak to you about helping him to share love and gentleness. *Pause.*

You can imagine Jesus is speaking very gently and lovingly to you. *Pause.*

Perhaps you will hear Jesus say something like this:

My little child,
I am so grateful for all the love you share. The more love you share, the more you open your heart to all of God's gentle love. How very much this helps the world around you. I will always be with you to help you share your love with all that God created. Thank you my little child. I love you very much. *Long Pause.*

Quietly in your mind, just let yourself feel how joyful it is to share your love with Jesus and the world around you. *Long pause.*

In a moment, we're going to open our eyes. But when we do, remember all the love we have to share, and how healing that love is to all the life God created in love. *Pause.*

When you're ready you can open your eyes.

Let us pray...

Thank you, Jesus, for helping us to share all the gentle love that lives deep inside our hearts. Help us to extend this love to everything around us, so our Earth will be more beautiful than ever. Amen.

My prayer to Jesus

9. WHY DO PEOPLE DIE?

Dear Jesus,

I'm very, very sad right now. Mom just told me
that my Grandpa died last night. I'm sure going
to miss him very much.

I know he was kind of old, Jesus, but I don't
really understand why people have to die.
Grandpa was real special. Once he taught me to
fly a kite with a long tail; and he always kept
butterscotch candies for me in his top dresser
drawer. I'm really going to miss him, Jesus.
I'm real sad, and I think I'm pretty angry, too.
Can you help me with this?

Love,

Doug

Dear Doug,

I understand how sad you are about your grandfather, and how much you'll miss all the fun you had together. But you know, Doug, you need to understand that there is a part of your grandfather that you'll always have, and that is his love.

God created each of us filled with love, and that love can never die, because it's forever. Every time you think a loving thought about your grandfather, you open up your heart to all the love and peace and joy inside of you. Your grandfather's love lies safely inside your heart and will be there forever. His love will always be with you, just as your love will always be with him.

No one's love can ever be lost, because God created the love inside us to live forever. Each of us has a special place inside our hearts for people we care about, and who care about us. Even if you can't share your bedtime stories with your grandfather now, you can still share your love, and that will be for always.

By the way, Doug, every time you begin to notice yourself thinking loving thoughts about your grandfather, it may be because he's thinking loving thoughts about you.

Love,

Jesus

Guided Meditation

Close your eyes and take a deep breath. *Pause.*

Take another breath, very deep this time, and exhale slowly. *Pause.*

Today we are going to discover that we can share the love deep inside of us, even with someone who might not be physically with us. *Pause.*

Quietly in your mind with your eyes closed, imagine yourself in a place that feels safe and secure. Anywhere you like, as long as it feels comfortable to you, and makes you feel happy and peaceful. *Pause.*

Just for a moment let yourself feel how safe and peaceful it is to be in your special place. *Pause.*

Imagine now, that you see Jesus. He's been waiting for you. If you like, you can let him hug you, or hold you. Or perhaps you just want to sit with him. He loves you so very much and it feels so very safe to be with him. *Pause.*

Now that you feel safe and loved with Jesus, perhaps you would like him to help you share all your love with someone else. Perhaps especially someone you miss who has died. Now together with Jesus think about how much you love that person. Let Jesus help you send him or her all your love. *Longer pause.*

Imagine that your love is like a beautiful ray of light. Imagine that light soaring higher and higher and farther and farther, as it travels happily to the heart of the person you're thinking of. *Long pause.*

Imagine too, that Jesus is helping you, as he sends all of his love along with yours. Imagine how bright those beautiful rays of light become as you join with Jesus in sending love. *Longer pause.*

Feel how wonderful it is to be with Jesus, and to share love along with him. Imagine, quietly, now in your mind that Jesus has something important he wants to tell you about love. He wants to help you learn that love is never lost, and that it's forever. *Longer pause.*

Perhaps you will hear Jesus say something like this:

My little child,
I love you so very much. Love is never lost. God created it in all of us forever. Each time you think a loving thought, you not only share it with me, but it dances in light and gently touches the heart of another in joy. How grateful I am for all your loving thoughts, and how very beautiful you are inside. I am always with you loving you forever. *Longer pause.*

Just let yourself feel how loved you are and how wonderful and safe you feel with Jesus, listening to his words. *Longer pause.*

In a moment we're going to open our eyes, and when we do we can remember Jesus is with us to help us send our love to people we care about. We can also remember that love is never lost, and every time we are loving we're learning all about the love inside us that God created. *Pause.*

Quietly, now when you're ready open your eyes.

||||||||||||||||||||||||||||||||||||||||||||||||||||||||||||||||||||||||||||||||||||||||||||||||||||||||||||||||||||||||||||||

Let us pray...

Jesus, help us to remember that love is forever, and all the love that God created is always safe inside our hearts. Thank you, Jesus, for helping us share all our loving thoughts and for reminding us how very beautiful we really are. Amen.

My prayer to Jesus

_____

_____

_____

_____

_____

Dear Jesus,

My parents both work, but my dad usually gets home before me. Sometimes, when he's running late, I come home from school to an empty house. I try real hard to be grown up when this happens. I try to take care of myself, but sometimes I'm a little scared.

It seems real neat to my friends that I have the house all to myself. But between you and me Jesus, it's more lonely than neat.

If my dad's not home, I turn on the TV and eat some cookies (fudge nut is my favorite). Sometimes I just play alone until he gets there.

I know you're pretty busy, Jesus, but could you help me not to be so scared and lonely on those days my dad is late?

Love,

Dear Chris,

Coming home to a house with no one in it can seem lonely and scary. First, it's important that you do everything you can to help yourself feel safe. You know not to open the door to anyone, and to have the phone number of an adult, if you need to talk.

You can help yourself not to feel afraid by reminding yourself that since you have the power to think of scary thoughts and believe in them, you also have the power to think thoughts that make you feel safe and loved, and to believe in that.

Anytime you're afraid or lonely, you can talk to me. Just turn off the TV or radio and get quiet. That will help you to listen better. If you're feeling lonely, you just forgot that I'm here. You just need to let me help you to remember. I'll be glad to listen to whatever is on your mind.

You need to remember, too, Chris, that true peace of mind and safety comes from deep inside of you. When you begin to remember all the love that we share, you'll begin to remember the true safety and peace you have inside of you that's always there.

Make sure, Chris, that you do all you can to take care of your body, and I'll do all I can to take care of your heart.

Love,
Jesus

Guided Meditation

Close your eyes and take a deep breath in and out. *Pause.*

Take another breath—very deep this time—in and out. *Pause.*

Today we are going to discover the true safety and peace that lies deep inside of us, and how to help ourselves to feel that safety and peace whenever we need to. *Pause.*

With your eyes closed, imagine yourself in your home in a room that feels particularly safe and comfortable. *Pause.*

It can be your bedroom, or a corner of the kitchen, or any place you feel safe and comfortable. *Pause.*

Let yourself feel how safe it is to be there. *Pause.*

Perhaps you can imagine your parents or a brother or sister somewhere else in the house. *Pause.*

Perhaps you can hear some of the noises of the house or the people outside doing the things they usually do. *Pause.*

Now quietly in your mind, invite Jesus into your comfortable place. *Pause.*

Imagine that he sits down next to you, and he smiles in joy that you asked him to come. *Pause.*

Imagine how safe it feels to be with Jesus, and how very, very much he loves you. *Longer pause.*

You can even imagine that all the noises in the house you heard before seem to quiet down and almost fade away. You're with Jesus now, and noises don't seem to matter. *Pause.*

Now with your eyes closed, while you feel safe with Jesus, tell him some thoughts you have that frighten you. *Pause.*

It's okay to tell him about whatever scares or troubles you. He loves you so very much, and he wants to help you with them. *Longer pause.*

Now that you've told Jesus all about some of your scary thoughts, imagine that he's going to help you with them. *Pause.*

Jesus wants you to share your fearful thoughts with him, so he can share all his loving, peaceful thoughts with you. *Pause.*

Perhaps you will hear Jesus say something like this:

My little child,
I love you, and I don't want you to ever feel afraid. Whenever you have a thought that frightens you, let me replace it with a loving thought that I so much want to share with you. Let me remind you of how very much I love you and how you're never truly alone. I am with you always and forever. *Longer pause.*

Let yourself rest with Jesus in his safety and his peace. *Longer pause.*

In a moment we're going to open our eyes, and when we do, let's remember we're not alone. Jesus is always with us to help us with our fearful thoughts. *Pause.*

Quietly, when you're ready, open your eyes.

Let us pray...

Thank you for helping us remember that you are always with us. Whenever we are afraid we know we can come to you and share your peace. Help us to remember that we are never really alone. Your love is always with us. Amen.

My prayer to Jesus

_____

_____

_____

_____

_____

11. MY PARENTS ARE GETTING DIVORCED!

Dear Jesus,

Last night my mother and father told me the most
awful thing I've ever heard in my whole life. They
told me that they are not going to live together
any more. I've heard of other kids parents doing this,
but I never thought that it would happen to me.

If my parents can decide not to live together any
more, I'm wondering if they might decide not to
want me anymore either.

I'm really scared, Jesus, about what is going to
happen to me. Please help me, because I'm awfully
worried.

Love,

Benjamin

Dear Benjamin,

I know how upset you are about your parents and how worried you must be. As people get older, Benjamin, they learn and grow, and that's healthy. But sometimes it happens that married couples find themselves learning and growing in two different directions. They are no longer able to share things or to talk to one another without fighting.

Sometimes married people then decide it's better to live apart rather than staying together. But that's really a decision they have made about each other, not about you. Even if your parents do get a divorce, they will still love you.

I want to remind you, too, Benjamin, that my love is always with you. I will always be with you through all the changes that occur in your life, even very difficult changes like divorce. So you are never really alone. My help is always with you.

By the way, Benjamin, one way to teach yourself that love can't be lost is by loving both your parents as much as you can. This will help you to remember that the love God created is always safe inside your heart. I will do all I can to help you remember this, too.

Love,

Jesus

Guided Meditation

Let's close our eyes and take a deep breath. Take another deep breath in, and exhale slowly. *Pause.*

With our eyes closed we're going to remember that Jesus' love is always with us, to help us through all the changes that occur in our lives. *Pause.*

Imagine yourself outside under a big beautiful tree on a beautiful spring day. The sun is high in the sky, and you can hear birds in the nearby trees and see small animals scampering about. *Pause.*

In your mind invite Jesus to be with you. Just quietly call his name and watch how quickly and gently he comes to be with you. *Pause.*

Jesus loves you so very much, and he is so glad that you want to be with him. Let yourself feel as safe and loved and peaceful as you can. *Pause.*

Now in a moment imagine that as you sit safely with Jesus, the season will begin to change. It won't really matter how things seem to change around you. You're with Jesus and you feel safe. *Pause.*

Imagine now that it's summer. Perhaps you are wearing lighter clothing and the sun is shining brighter and warmer. Feel how loved and safe you are with Jesus, in spite of the changes around you. *Pause.*

Now imagine that the season changes again. The leaves on the tree are turning colors and the weather is getting cooler. *Pause.*

Now imagine that it's winter and you are dressed in warm clothes, and perhaps you can even see some snow. You can sit with Jesus and watch the snowflakes fall onto the ground. *Longer pause.*

It doesn't matter how much things are changing outside. Deep inside your heart and mind Jesus is there loving you, and helping you feel comfortable and safe. *Pause.*

Now quietly in your mind imagine that Jesus has something to tell you about change. He wants you to know that his love and care for you is always the same, no matter how things seem to change around you. *Pause.*

Perhaps you will hear Jesus say something like this:

My little child,
I love you very much. I am always with you helping you to feel comfortable and safe, and to remember all the love and peace that lives gently in your heart. No matter how much change takes place around you, my love and care is always the same. I love you completely and always. Whenever you need to feel safe in the midst of change, let me help you remember all the love and safety that lies inside your heart that God created. *Longer pause.*

Quietly in your mind let yourself feel how much Jesus loves you and always cares for you. *Pause.*

In a moment we're going to open our eyes. When we do let's remember that Jesus is always with us to help us feel safe through whatever changes occur in our lives. His love and peace are always with us. *Pause.*

Now when you're ready, open your eyes.

Let us pray...

Help us, Jesus, to remember that your gentle love is always constant, no matter what changes occur around us. Help us to remember that we are welcome to come to you whenever we need to. Amen.

My prayer to Jesus

Dear Jesus,

I have a secret that I'm too ashamed to tell anyone. But since it's really bothering me, I'll tell you.

When my parents take me to church I don't understand any of the things that the priest is doing. He uses words I never hear anywhere else, and none of them make any sense to me.

My parents say that they always feel better after going to church, but I just feel bored. Then I feel guilty about being bored.

My secret is that I don't want to go to church any more, and I don't understand why I always have to go. Does this make me a bad person?

Could you please help me with this problem?

Love,

Adam

P.S. I hope you're not angry at me because I don't like going to church.

Dear Adam,

I'm so happy that you trust me enough to tell me your secret. No, Adam, your feelings do not make you a bad person, and I could never be angry with you for sharing them.

I'll bet there are a lot of children who, like you, think that church is sometimes boring. It's easy to feel bored when you don't understand something. As you grow older, you will understand the words and actions better, and you will know why going to church is a very important way for you to praise and worship God.

Even now, Adam, when you don't understand something, ask your parents to explain it to you. Little by little those "difficult" words and actions will become an important part of your own prayer and worship.

Remember, every time you talk to me or to God you are praying. Did you know that even writing me this letter is a way of praying? It makes me happy to know that you feel safe enough and trust me enough to ask me for help with your problem. Asking for help is a way of praying, too!

I'll always be here for you, Adam, and I'll always love you.

Love,
Jesus

Guided Meditation

With your eyes closed take a deep breath and exhale slowly. Take another deep breath, and let out all the air. *Pause.*

Today with our eyes closed we are going to learn about prayer, how God hears our prayers, and is always there to help us. *Pause.*

With your eyes closed, imagine yourself in a beautiful little chapel. *Pause.*

It is quiet, and very, very peaceful inside, and there is nobody there but you. *Pause.*

Perhaps your little chapel has stained glass windows and the sunlight makes everything sparkle inside. *Pause.*

You can imagine yourself sitting down in a comfortable spot in the chapel, and feel how very still, peaceful, and safe you feel. *Pause.*

Imagine now that you see Jesus. His gentle eyes sparkle as he smiles at you. You can tell how very, very much he loves you. *Longer pause.*

Imagine that Jesus sits down next to you. He loves you and wants to be with you. *Pause.*

If you like, you can let Jesus hold your hand. Or you can even rest your head on his chest. *Pause.*

Just let yourself experience how very peaceful it is to be with Jesus and how very much he loves you. *Longer pause.*

Now Jesus wants to teach you about prayer. He wants you to learn how very loved you are, and how much he treasures you. *Pause.*

In your mind, tell Jesus how you feel about going to Mass. What about it do you find hard? What about it do you like? You can tell him about your true feelings. *Longer pause.*

Now that you have told Jesus about your true feelings and concerns, imagine that he wants to answer you. *Pause.*

He wants to let you know that he will help you if you just trust him. *Pause.*

Imagine now that Jesus begins to answer you very gently. Perhaps he will say something like this:

My little child,
I love you so very much. I am always here to answer all your prayers. I answer prayers by giving peace. If you let me, I will help you to discover how to help yourself with whatever is disturbing you. Perhaps one day, when you are feeling peaceful, the answer to your question will come to you. Trust that I am always with you and always helping you. I love you very much. *Long pause.*

Let yourself experience how very much Jesus loves you and how he is always trying to help you to feel his peace. *Longer pause.*

In a moment we are going to open our eyes. When we do, remember how much Jesus loves us and that he will answer all of our prayers with his love. *Pause.*

Now when you're ready, quietly open your eyes.

Let us pray...

Help us to learn that prayers are answered with your peace. Whenever we are quiet and still, we can learn by listening to you that you are trying to answer our concerns with your love. Amen.

My prayer to Jesus

_____

_____

_____

_____

_____

13. HALLOWEEN COSTUMES SCARE ME!

Dear Jesus,

Halloween is coming soon, and I really like trick-or-treating and parties, and most of all I like the candy!

I like wearing a costume and making people guess who I am. There is a big something that I don't like about Halloween though.

Sometimes other kids dress up in costumes that look like the monsters in my nightmares. These really give me the creeps. I mean, I know that there are just regular people inside the costumes, but their masks and make-up look so real that sometimes I forget they're just costumes.

Could you help me with this problem? I like Halloween, but I'm tired of being afraid of parts of it, and I don't want other kids to think I'm a sissy.

Love,

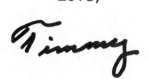
Timmy

Dear Timmy,

I would be happy to help you look at something that seems frightening and see it in a different way. That is why I'm here, to remind anyone that asks for my help, that there is another way to see scary things.

You see, Timmy, you and I, and everyone you'll ever see or meet in the world, are still exactly the way God created us. We are beautiful, loving creations that are loved by God for longer than forever. God's love is bigger than the world you live in, and it lasts for always and always.

Now when people become afraid they act in many different ways. They may become angry or sad. They might yell, cry, or sulk, or even try to scare other people. Did you know that being afraid is like wearing one of those scary costumes? Because even though someone might be yelling, crying, or sulking; inside (or underneath their costume of fear) they are still the same loving person that God created.

So, Timmy, this year when you go trick-or-treating and see a costume that reminds you of nightmare monsters, instead of being afraid, let that costume also remind you of all the silly masks people wear every day. Remember that beneath those masks are people that God loves!

Love,
Jesus

Guided Meditation

Let's close our eyes and take a deep breath and then exhale slowly. *Pause.*

Take another deep breath and exhale. With your eyes closed imagine a beautiful meadow, filled with green grass and lovely flowers. *Pause.*

In the middle of the meadow is a beautiful large tree that gives lots of shade. Imagine now Jesus is sitting under the tree. He's waiting to spend time with you because he loves you. *Pause.*

You can look at Jesus and see all the love in his eyes, and all the joy he has to share with you. *Pause.*

If you like, you can let him hold you, or you can just sit with him quietly under the beautiful tree. Imagine whatever feels comfortable and makes you feel safe and secure. *Pause.*

Now that you are with Jesus and feel safe, perhaps you can talk to him about someone who upsets you, or someone you are afraid of. Jesus will help you to deal with your fear and help you to feel better. *Pause.*

Imagine you see the person who upsets you or scares you off in a distance. *Pause.*

It's all right to let that person come a little closer if you like. Allow him or her in your mind to come as close as you feel comfortable. Jesus is with you and you can feel safe. *Pause.*

As you sit safely with Jesus imagine a beautiful golden light all around Jesus and you. *Pause.*

Feel how peaceful this light is, and how loving. *Pause.*

Now imagine that golden light surrounding the person who has upset you. You can see the person begin to feel the glow of the light, and become more peaceful and loving. *Longer pause.*

Underneath all the anger and upset that person seems to have, is all the love that God created. You both had forgotten it was there. *Pause.*

Perhaps you can let Jesus help you to understand this person better. Jesus will also help you to forgive him or her. *Pause.*

Quietly, in your mind listen to what Jesus has to say about forgiveness. *Pause.*

Perhaps Jesus will say something like this:

My lovely child,
Sometimes people act in ways that upset you. But you can remember that is because they have forgotten all the love inside of them that God created. But you can help them remember, even when they forget. I'm always here to help you to remember, too! I'm always with you, and I love you always. *Longer pause.*

In a few moments we're going to open our eyes. But we can remember that the love God created is within everyone, even though people sometimes forget about it. *Pause.*

We can remember Jesus is always with us to help us to learn that God's love is forever. *Pause.*

Quietly, when you're ready, open your eyes.

|||||||||||||||||||||||||||||||||||||||||||||||||||||||||||||||||||||||||||||||||||||||||||||||||||||||||||||||||||||||||||||||||||||||||||||||||||

Let us pray...

Jesus, please help us to remember all of the love inside of us that God created. Help us to remember, too, that everyone has God's gift of love, and love was created to be shared.

Amen.

My prayer to Jesus

_____

_____

_____

_____

_____

14. MY FAMILY FIGHTS TOO MUCH

Dear Jesus,

Pretty soon it will be Christmas and then New Year's.

I want to like these holidays; I really do. But the families on television always seem to have a much better time than we do at home. I watch them on TV laughing together and helping each other, and being glad that they are a family. I feel sad when I see that, because that's never how things are with my family.

It seems like someone here always gets angry on a holiday and starts yelling and fighting about things. Then no one speaks to anyone else. I always end up wishing the holiday was over, or that it had never come.

Why is my family like this? Are we the only ones who aren't happy together?

Maybe if I were a better child, the people in my house would be happier. Sometimes I know it's all my fault, even if they don't say so.

Could you please help me with this problem? I sure would appreciate it.

Love,

Jeff

Dear Jeff,

Holidays can be joyful times, but for many people they are difficult times, too. Many children and adults feel cheated about how little happiness they get on Christmas and other holidays.

First of all, Jeff, real families are never as happy and perfect as TV families. Those families aren't real; they're just characters some writers made up. People in real families sometimes act out their feelings by fighting or sulking, or acting in ways that seem difficult.

They do this because they forget that real happiness doesn't come from anything outside of ourselves, like how many presents we get. Real happiness comes from that special wonderful place inside of us that God created, the place where love is allowed to live and grow. That's really what the holidays should be all about.

It's not your fault if people in your house are unhappy, Jeff. They just forgot where love is, and they're looking in the wrong place. But even if they choose to be unhappy, you and I can celebrate together. You can remember during the holidays and always that I am with you and you're never alone, even if things in your house don't always go the way you want them to. I'm always with you, loving you. You don't have to be or do anything different for me to love you. I've always loved you, and I always will.

Love,

Jesus

Guided Meditation

Close your eyes and be very still. Today we are going to visit once again that special place that we all have inside of us, a place where all of God's love waits for you to remember that it is there. *Pause.*

Jesus lives in this place of love inside of you. *Pause.*

Can you see Jesus smiling at you? His love is always safe and always there. In this special place your love for him is always safe and always there, too! *Pause.*

Imagine a beautiful big tree. Its branches reach higher, higher, higher than the clouds in the blue, blue sky. *Pause.*

Its leaves are deep, cool, and green. They shade a soft spot for you to sit and rest. *Pause.*

Imagine that Jesus is sitting beneath that big, wonderful tree. You can sit down next to him and put your head on his shoulder if you want to. *Pause.*

Can you feel how much Jesus loves you? No matter who you are, what you have done, or what you haven't done, no matter what you look like, Jesus' love is always there for you. *Longer pause.*

Jesus is always there to listen to whatever you would like to share with him. You can tell him about things that make you happy, or you can tell him about something that makes you sad. You can tell him anything at all that you want to. *Pause.*

Quietly, in your mind, now tell Jesus something you would like him to know. *Longer pause.*

Imagine Jesus putting his arms around you and holding you. Perhaps he will say something like this to you:

My dearest child,
No matter what you tell me, I love you forever and always. I'm sorry when other people make you unhappy, but remember that you can always talk to me. I'm always with you, loving you and listening to you. *Longer pause.*

In a minute, you're going to open your eyes. And when you do, remember that quiet, special place inside of you where you can tell Jesus anything that you would like him to know. He will always be there to listen. Remember that no matter what you tell Jesus, good or bad he will always love you.

Now slowly begin to open your eyes.

Let us pray...

Jesus, it makes us feel happy to know that we can share anything with you that we want. And it makes us feel extra happy to know how much you love us, no matter what. Thank you for loving us. Amen

My prayer to Jesus

_____

_____

_____

_____

_____

15. WHY AREN'T PEOPLE HAPPY?

Dear Jesus,

I've been thinking a lot lately about the real
meaning of Christmas. I know that you came to bring
love and peace into the world and to teach all
of us to be like you. I know you want people to be
happy. But I don't think we have learned these
lessons very well.

I hear grown-ups talking all the time about "how
bad things are." Television is filled with sad
stories of people fighting and getting hurt.
Jesus, there's so much fighting and sadness in the
world! Where is the love and peace you came to
bring? Why aren't people happy?

Sometimes I think that maybe you're disappointed
in the way we all behave, or that you're even sorry
you ever came among us. That makes me feel very
sad.

Sometimes I wonder if you're disappointed in me,
too.

Love,

Caitlin

Dear Caitlin,

Sometimes people do act in ways that seem to be very cruel. But I know that is because deep inside of them they are afraid. People forget that they may be different on the outside, but that deep inside they are all created with the same love. God loves all of them equally, and forever, and that is the message I came to give the world.

It is because people forget all the love that lives inside of them that they become afraid and unhappy. Sometimes people even think that others are loved more than they are. So they will fight to get back what they think they have lost.

But love can never be lost, Caitlin. My love is always with you. You could never disappoint me because all that I see is the love and beauty inside of you. No matter what you or anyone else may think or believe, I'll always love you.

No, I am not sorry I came. Each time anyone remembers the love inside of them they are remembering me and celebrating Christmas in their hearts.

This is the meaning of Christmas. It is celebrating and sharing the love inside all of us and forgiving others when they forget.

Love,

Jesus

Guided Meditation

Close your eyes and slowly take a deep breath in. Exhale slowly. *Pause.*

Take another deep breath in, and out. *Pause.*

Deep inside of us is a wonderful place of love that God created. Let's be very quiet, and feel that love. *Pause.*

Here in this peaceful, loving place, all of our worries seem to disappear, because we are remembering how very much God loves us. *Pause.*

With your eyes closed, imagine that you see Jesus. *Pause.*

Look into his eyes. Can you see how much he loves you? *Pause.*

If you want to, you can let Jesus hold you for a while, or you can just sit down next to him. Imagine whatever feels most comfortable, because Jesus loves you, and he wants you to feel happy and safe. *Longer pause.*

Jesus has something he wants to tell you. Something special that will mean a great deal to you. Imagine Jesus telling you something loving that makes you feel warm and wonderful.

Listen to him speak lovingly to you in your mind. *Longer pause.*

It feels so good to be with Jesus because he loves you very much. Now that Jesus has told you something, perhaps you would like to tell him something special, quietly in your mind. You can tell him anything that you would like to share with him. He loves you, and he's always there to listen. Quietly, tell Jesus in your mind something you want him to know. *Longer pause.*

Imagine Jesus is still with you, loving you. Perhaps he is saying something like this to you:

My little child,
I love you so very much. I am always with you. Whenever you need to, you can come to this quiet place, and I will be glad to tell you how much I care about you, and how much you mean to me. Whenever you need to, you can come here. I'll always be waiting for you. I love you my child, and I'll be here with you always. *Pause.*

Let's spend another moment or two feeling how good it is to be with Jesus. *Pause.*

We're going to open our eyes soon. When we do, we can remember that Jesus loves us, and whenever we need to we can come to this quiet place and talk with him. He loves us and wants us to feel safe and happy.

Slowly open your eyes.

Let us pray...

Jesus, thank you for always being there for us. We know that whenever we need to, we can come and be with you. You'll always help us to feel safe and happy. Amen.

My prayer to Jesus

Dear Jesus,

Today I heard a story about the three wise men.
They came to bring you beautiful gifts to celebrate
your birthday.

I liked the story of the three wise men, and I thought
how nice it would be if I could give you a birthday
gift, too.

I looked around at all my stuff, like my books, my
baseball bat, my bicycle, and my lucky baseball cap.
But I don't think you can use any of this stuff.

Now I feel bad. Maybe the wise men were just special
and lucky enough to bring you just the right
presents. But I wish I could give you a special
birthday gift, too.

                                        Love,

                              Robbie

Dear Robbie,

It is true that the wise men came and brought me gifts a long time ago. But that alone didn't make them special.

Robbie, you don't realize it, but you give me gifts, too, ones that I treasure with all my heart. Each thought of love, each little kindness, every smile is a gift to me, and how grateful I am for all the love you give.

I rejoice each time you're happy, and I smile each time you remember the love inside of you that God created.

Please don't ever feel that you have nothing to give me. Your love for me and everyone else is the most precious gift I could ever receive, and how grateful I am for all your loving thoughts.

Love,

Jesus

Guided Meditation

Close your eyes now and be very still.

Take a deep breath in; then slowly exhale. Take another deep breath in and slowly exhale. *Pause.*

Today we are going to remember the special place of love inside of us that God created. *Pause.*

This is a familiar place to you, because you've been there before. Now quietly feel that special, wonderful place of love that you have visited before. *Pause.*

With your eyes closed, think of some special place that you would like to spend quiet time alone with Jesus. It can be a park, or by the seashore, or any place that you enjoy. *Pause.*

Now imagine that Jesus is next to you. You feel so safe and loved. When you're with Jesus you have nothing to worry about, because you know how much he loves you. *Pause.*

See Jesus smiling at you? His eyes are soft and gentle. He puts his arm around your shoulder, and that makes you feel warm and loved. *Pause.*

Now Jesus would like to tell you something wonderful, so listen carefully.

My dear little child,
Soon you will celebrate my birthday. And in the spirit of that day, I would like to give you gifts. My gifts to you will be my peace, my joy, and my love, and these are the only gifts you will ever truly need. If you should ever forget that I have given you these gifts, I will always be here in your heart to remind you. My peace will comfort you whenever you are afraid. My joy will laugh with you when you are happy with yourself and with others. And my love will be your strength and your guidance. These gifts will remain in your heart now, on Christmas, and for all of your life. *Longer pause.*

Now decide what gift you would like to give Jesus for his birthday. It can be a gift of your love, the gift of your happiness, the gift of your smiles shared with others, or the gift of your gratitude for the beautiful gifts Jesus has given you. *Pause.*

Now quietly, in your mind, tell Jesus what gifts you would like to give him for Christmas. *Pause.*

Jesus is so happy with the gifts you have given him for his birthday! Imagine that he is giving you a big, wonderful hug, and thanking you for your special gifts. *Pause.*

In a moment you will open your eyes, and when you do, you will always remember the gifts that Jesus has given you for this Christmas and always. *Pause.*

Now slowly open your eyes.

Let us pray...

Thank you, Jesus, for the gifts of your peace, love, and joy. We will always know that they are in our hearts, and that we can share them with others.
Happy Birthday! Amen.

My prayer to Jesus

17. DOES GOD ALWAYS FORGIVE?

Dear Jesus,

The New Year just started and everyone celebrated.
I got to stay up late with all the grown-ups. I had a
noisemaker and a hat, and we all yelled Happy New
Year real loud.

All the grown-ups talked about their promises to
try and change things they don't like about
themselves. They called it "turning a new leaf" and
starting over again. My Dad explained to me that the
New Year is like starting fresh, almost like when I
start a new grade in school.

So I wondered, does God start fresh with us too?
Does God ever turn a new leaf, and forget about those
times when we weren't so nice? Does God always
forgive me?

I'm a little worried about this. I know I'm not
always so good, but will God give me another chance?

Love,

P.S. Do we ever run out of chances?

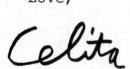

Dear Celita,

Happy New Year, little one! Yes, many people choose a New Year to change bad habits or begin good ones.

It's a wonderful idea, a New Year "fresh start." I have another idea for you though. You can have a fresh start or turn a new leaf with each and every thought you have. You can decide with each thought whether you will allow your kindness and laughter and love to show in your relationships with other people, or you can decide that you will not.

God understands how difficult it is to always respond to others with love. God also knows that sometimes you forget that you have everything you need, and are especially loved—just like everyone else in the world.

But God knows, too, that every person needs lots and lots of chances to try to remember these things. So, Celita, everyone has as many chances as they need, their whole life through, because God knows that sooner or later they will remember how very much they are loved and that they will absolutely want to share that love with everyone.

Love,

Jesus

Guided Meditation

Let's close our eyes and come to quiet. *Pause.*

Take a deep breath in, and then let it out. Then take another deep breath in and exhale slowly. *Pause.*

Quietly in your mind, with your eyes closed, imagine that you have come home from school and found your favorite room at home decorated for a party. You can imagine it as bright and colorful as you like. *Pause.*

This is a special party room, because this is a special party. This is a quiet celebration. Just you and Jesus will be there. *Pause.*

Quietly now, with your eyes closed, imagine Jesus in your beautiful party room. He wants to celebrate all his love for you and all your love for him. *Pause.*

You can imagine feeling as close to Jesus as you like. *Longer pause.*

Perhaps you would like to tell Jesus something you need help with, perhaps something about yourself you would like to change, or a bad habit you would like to stop. *Pause.*

Quietly, in your mind, tell Jesus whatever it is that you want him to help you with. *Longer pause.*

Now that you've told Jesus what it is you want help with, it's okay to listen to what he has to say to you. *Longer pause.*

Perhaps Jesus said something like this:

Beautiful child,
I love you. I'll be glad to help you with whatever

bothers you. I'll be happy to help you to try to change anything about yourself you don't like. You can remember all the love inside of you that God created. That love and gentleness is what you really are. I'll help you to remember that ~~as much as you need me to~~. I'll always be with you. *Longer pause.*

Quietly, in your mind, just let yourself feel how wonderful it is to be loved by Jesus. *Pause.*

In a few moments, you will open your eyes. You can take with you all of Jesus' love into the world. You can remember that he's here to help you and he'll never ever leave you. Whenever you need him, he'll be here waiting for you. *Pause.*

Quietly, open your eyes.

Let us pray...

Jesus, thank you for teaching us to know that you are always with us to help us to change whatever feelings trouble us, and to help us to see ourselves in a different way. Amen.

My prayer to Jesus

_____

_____

_____

_____

_____

18.   WHAT SHOULD I GIVE UP?

Dear Jesus,

Lent is coming and my religion teacher talked to
us about giving up something for Lent that we love.
I love a lot of things, Jesus. Maybe I could
give up candy or ice cream, because they are my
favorites, but actually I like watching cartoons
on Saturday mornings just as much. I really am
having a hard time deciding.

What do you think? What would you like me to give
up? I want you to be proud of me, and I want to
make you happy. So I'll just wait for you to tell
me before I decide.

Love,

Joey

Dear Joey,

You ask what I would like you to give up. You might
be a little surprised by my answer. You see, Joey, it
really doesn't matter so much whether you give up
candy, ice cream, or cartoons. What matters much more is
that you give up all the thoughts that hurt you and
cause you pain, and all the thoughts that make you
unhappy.

I love you so very much, and I want you to be happy. I
will do everything I can to help you feel better when
you're unhappy.

You can think of Lent as a time to give me all your
hurtful and angry thoughts, and any thoughts and
feelings that make you feel bad inside. You can talk
to me about your unhappy thoughts and feelings any time.
When you do, I will help you to see what is happening
inside of you in a different way, and that will help you
to feel better.

By the way, Joey, also remember that I always love you,
and you don't have to do anything special to make me
happy. Your love makes me happy, and I can see that your
heart is full of love. I am happy just being with
you, even when you forget to remember that I'm here.

Love,

Jesus

Guided Meditation

Close your eyes and come to quiet. Take a deep breath in and then let it out. Take another deep breath, and let it all out. *Pause.*

This is the place where love is. It is also the place where you know you are loved very much, forever and always. *Pause.*

Now imagine in this quiet place of love, that you see Jesus. *Pause.*

He is walking toward you to welcome you. He loves you so very much. *Pause.*

Imagine that you and Jesus sit down together. You can sit next to him if you like, or you can sit on his lap if you want to. He loves you and he wants you to feel comfortable and safe. *Longer pause.*

Now that you are feeling close to Jesus and very safe, maybe you would like to talk to him. *Pause.*

Talk to him about your worries and concerns or about thoughts that make you feel unhappy. These can be angry or scary thoughts, or anything that upsets you. Jesus would like to help you with them because he wants you to feel better. *Pause.*

Quietly now, with your eyes closed, tell Jesus whatever upsets you. He will listen because he loves you so very much. *Longer pause.*

Now that you have told Jesus your concerns, he would like to help you. He loves you and wants you to feel happy inside. *Pause.*

Imagine Jesus is speaking to you. He has something he would like to say to you that will make you feel better. *Pause.*

Perhaps Jesus said something like this to you:

My little child,
I love you so very much. Whenever you are upset, let me help you with whatever is troubling you. I am always here loving you. I will try to help you to feel better and to know that you're never alone. I'm always with you. You're my little child for always. *Longer pause.*

It's okay now to just let yourself remember how safe it feels to be with Jesus. He loves you and wants you to talk to him any time you need to. He wants to help you feel happy and peaceful inside. *Longer pause.*

In a moment you're going to open your eyes. When you do, you can take with you all the safe, warm, loving feelings you received from Jesus.

You can remember that Jesus is waiting for you to come to him. He loves you and he is always with you.

Quietly now, open your eyes.

Let us pray...

Jesus, help us to remember the love inside of us that lasts forever. Teach us that you are always here to help us with our thoughts of anger and fear and that with your love we can find a better way. Amen.

My prayer to Jesus

19. WHY DID JESUS DIE?

Dear Jesus,

Easter is almost here. I like Easter because I know that spring is coming, and I really like spring.

But there is also something that I don't like about Easter. Good Friday comes right before it. I don't like the story of how people nailed you to a cross and killed you.

It makes me feel so sad every time I hear about it. I saw a movie about this on TV, and you looked so awful. My religion teacher told me that you died for our sins. But could I have ever done anything so bad that you had to die because of it? If it really is my fault, then I don't like myself very much.

Please help me.

Love,

Abigail

Dear Abigail,

I always tried to teach people about God's love, but some people became very frightened when they heard me teach. You see, Abigail, they didn't feel very good about themselves inside, and so they had a hard time listening, and really believing that God loved them, too.

My message about God's love frightened them, so they mistakenly thought that if they killed me, and got rid of me, they would also get rid of God's love. But they were wrong.

God's love is always there for everyone, all the time. As a matter of fact, that is the real message of Easter: that God's love can't be killed or gotten rid of. Love is forever and nothing can ever change that.

So when you think of Easter, think of the happy, joyful message that my love, like God's, is always with you and will never leave you. This love is in your heart, and I will always be with you to help you remember all the love inside of you that God created for you to share with everyone.

Love,

Jesus

Guided Meditation

Let's close our eyes and take a deep breath. In and then out. Now take another deep breath and exhale slowly. *Pause.*

Now with our eyes closed, we're going to visit that special, lovely place within us that God created, that special place of love. *Pause.*

Imagine a beautiful garden. It's full of the most wonderful flowers you have ever seen. They are bright red, deep blue, lovely pink, and all shades of any color you can imagine. *Pause.*

Perhaps this garden has cool little shade trees surrounding it and a little brook on its side. Are there any birds singing in your garden? Are there little animals? *Pause.*

You are free to imagine your garden to be as beautiful as you like. *Pause.*

Now imagine Jesus is in your garden. He's waiting for you to come and visit with him. *Pause.*

You can look at him and see how much he loves you. His eyes are kind, and he is so very happy to be with you. *Longer pause.*

You can sit next to him and let him hold your hand. Or if you like, you can let him hold you very close. Imagine whatever makes you feel most comfortable and happy. Jesus loves you and wants you to feel happy and safe. *Longer pause.*

Now that you're feeling safe and happy, perhaps you would like to tell Jesus about something that upsets you, or a person who hasn't treated you very nicely. *Pause.*

It's okay to tell Jesus everything you feel about that person. Jesus loves you and he wants to listen. *Longer pause.*

Now that you've told Jesus all about your feelings, perhaps you can listen to him. He loves you and he wants to help you. *Pause.*

Imagine in your mind that Jesus will answer you, and help you with your feelings. He loves you so very much and he wants you to feel better. *Pause.*

Perhaps Jesus said something like this:

My sweet child,
I love you so much. I know that you may feel upset over this person. But try to remember that when people act in ways you don't like, it is because they're upset inside. Sometimes, when people are hurting inside they say or act in ways that are not very nice. I will help you to remember that. It's okay to tell them how you feel. It's also okay to try and forgive them. I will help you to do both. I'm always here to help you. I love you. *Longer pause.*

Now that you've listened to Jesus, imagine he's giving you a hug, if you would like one. *Pause.*

In a moment, we're going to open our eyes. But we can bring the lovely experience we had in our beautiful garden back with us.

When you're ready, open your eyes.

||||||||||||||||||||||||||||||||||||||||||||||||||||||||||||||||||||||||||||||||||||||||||||||||||||||||||||||||||||||||||

Let us pray...

Jesus, thank you for helping us to understand that anger comes from fear, and that fearful people have forgotten about the love inside of them. Help us to remember that you are always with us. Amen.

My prayer to Jesus

_____

_____

_____

_____

_____

Dear Jesus,

My friends Jason, Randy, and I were talking about Pentecost because we learned about it in religion class. I know that's when the Holy Spirit came to the apostles and they were speaking in tongues. Jason said that he was scared, because it could happen to him. He's afraid he might get the Holy Spirit, and then he'd speak another language and no one would understand him.

I know this idea is pretty silly, Jesus, but I told him I would write you a letter because he was afraid to ask you himself. Will the Holy Spirit come to us and make us do weird things?

Love,

Danny

Dear Danny,

I'm glad you are learning about Pentecost in religion class, and I understand how afraid you can be of what you don't understand. So let me explain things so you won't be frightened.

The Holy Spirit is the gentle voice of love inside you. That voice and presence is always with you, loving you and helping you in a very tender way.

The Holy Spirit will never frighten you or come in a way that you don't understand. Whenever you hear this loving gentle voice, it will always make you feel peaceful and happy inside. It will help you to remember all the love that you have, that is safe within your heart.

Because the apostles experienced the love of the Holy Spirit in a particular way, doesn't mean that you will have the same experience, especially if it frightens you.

The Holy Spirit helps each person feel better, and will give each person just what each needs. Do you wonder how I know this? It's because the Holy Spirit is really my own spirit. When the Spirit speaks to your heart and loves you, it is me speaking to you and loving you. So remember that I'm always with you, just as the Holy Spirit is, to help you remember the love inside of you.

Love,

Jesus

Guided Meditation

Close your eyes and take a deep breath. Take another breath, in and out. *Pause.*

Today with our eyes closed, we're going to experience the gentleness of the Holy Spirit's love, which is really the love of Jesus. *Pause.*

With your eyes closed, quietly in your mind imagine yourself in a beautiful orchard. The trees are filled with beautiful ripening fruit. *Pause.*

Imagine the early morning sun shining on your face. *Pause.*

If you like, you can sit under one of the trees and feel the soft, gentle breeze on your face. *Pause.*

Now imagine that the Holy Spirit's love is as gentle and soft as the breeze you are feeling. *Pause.*

Imagine the voice of the Holy Spirit that is soft, warm, and loving, saying to you, "I love you." *Long Pause.*

Now imagine that you no longer hear "I love you" just in the breeze, but you can hear these words deep inside your heart. *Long pause.*

Imagine the gentle voice of love in your heart whispering "I love you" over and over again. *Long pause.*

Feel how warm this makes your heart, and how wonderful it feels to know the gentle love of the Holy Spirit is with you. *Long pause.*

Now imagine in your mind that you see Jesus. He comes toward you with his arms open. If you like you can run into his arms and let him hug you. *Long pause.*

Jesus loves you, and is happy that you want to listen to the voice of his Spirit. *Pause.*

Just for a moment, let yourself experience how safe and loved you feel, and how happy you are that love is always with you. You know now that you can hear the Holy Spirit's gentle voice whenever you choose to listen because it is also the voice of Jesus. *Long pause.*

Listen as Jesus speaks to you about this. Perhaps you will hear him say something like this:

My little child,
The voice of love is always with you. This voice is completely gentle and always loving and kind. The Holy Spirit, my own spirit, will help you remember all the love that is forever inside your heart. The Spirit knows what you need to feel better, and will always speak to you in a way that will bring you peace. Through my Holy Spirit I am with you always, helping you to know how very loved you are. *Long pause.*

Quietly, in your mind, let yourself feel all the gentleness of Jesus' love and peace. *Long pause.*

In a moment we're going to open our eyes. When we do, remember that love is always speaking to us in perfect gentleness, and we can hear the Spirit of Jesus whenever we choose to listen. *Pause.*

Now when you're ready, quietly open your eyes.

||||||||||||||||||||||||||||||||||||||||||||||||||||||||||||||||||||||||||||||||||||||||||||||||||||||||||||||||||||||||||||||||||||||||||||||||||||||||||||||||||||||||||||||||||||||||

Let us pray...

Thank you, Jesus, for reminding us that the gentle voice of the Holy Spirit is always with us. Help us to listen to this loving voice whenever we are afraid.
Remind us that this love lives in our hearts forever. Amen.

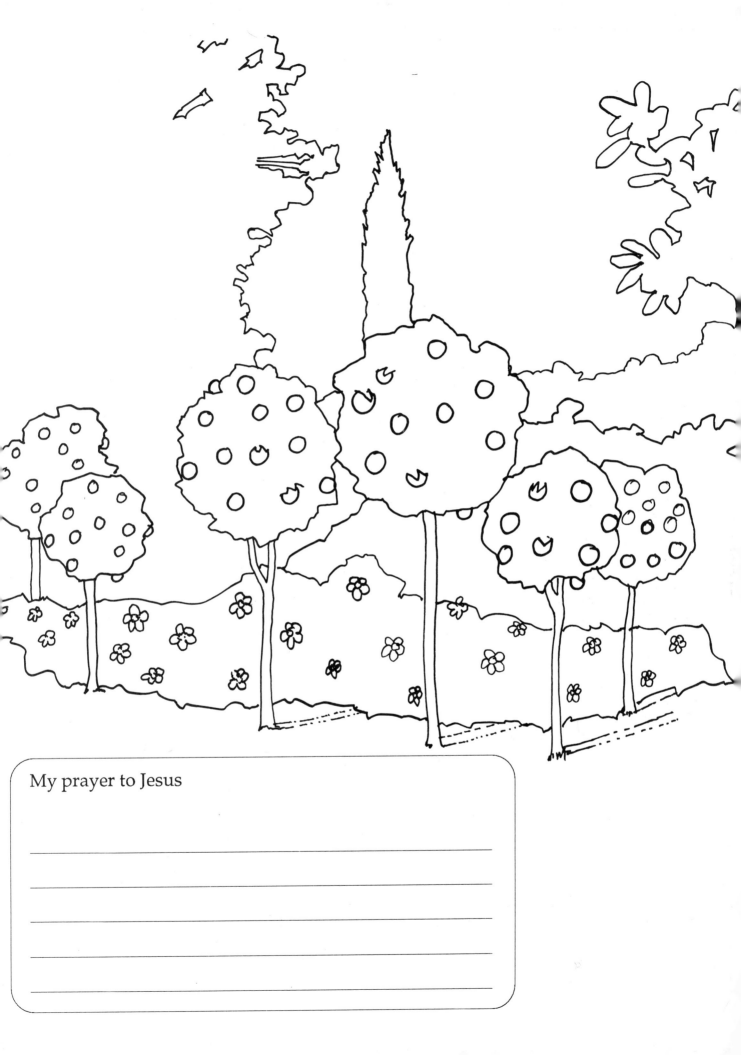

My prayer to Jesus

More excellent resources for young children...

Four of the best-loved stories from the popular video series "Holydays and Holidays" are now available as colorful children's books. These values-laden stories are:

- ◆ **CHARLES CATERPILLAR,** who learns that change/growth is unsettling, inevitable and promising
- ◆ **EDNA EAGLE,** whose sadness, love and loyalty are the themes of this bitter-sweet story
- ◆ **PRISCILLA TADPOLE,** who discovers that new beginnings lead to added richness in life
- ◆ **PACO PUMPKIN,** who finds that being different is a gift in itself

These books help prepare children for life's challenges—change, growth, friendship, discovery. The delightful characters help young children identify with these inevitabilities and prepare them for being open to the discoveries and possibilities life presents them. In addition, the books will provide endless hours of sheer enjoyment.

The authors of these books are experienced educators and writers, and the illustrators capture the very essence of the characters' personalities with bright, colorful, often touching artwork. An "Adult Page" in each book suggests ways for parents and teachers to stimulate further thought and discussion based on the stories.

The books are accessible to young hands, in a format 9 inches wide by 6 inches deep. The large size type encourages children to begin recognizing letters and words and the books are printed on a durable paper that will stand up to lots of use.

Charles Caterpillar by James Haas, ISBN: 0-89622-530-5, 9" X 6", Paper, $4.95 (order C-79)

Edna Eagle by Gwen Costello, ISBN: 0-809622-528-3, 9" X 6", Paper, $4.95 (order C-80)

Priscilla Tadpole by Gwen Costello, ISBN: 0-89622-527-5, 9" x 6", Paper, $4.95 (order C-82)

Paco Pumpkin by James Haas, ISBN: 0-89622-529-1, 9" X 6", Paper, $4.95 (order C-81)

Available at religious bookstores or from
TWENTY-THIRD PUBLICATIONS
P.O. Box 180 • Mystic, CT 06355 • 1-800-321-0411